JEFF BEZOS

BY SARA GREEN

BELLWETHER MEDIA • MINNEAPOLIS, MN

Jump into the cockpit and take flight with Pilot books. Your journey will take you on high-energy adventures as you learn about all that is wild, weird, fascinating, and fun!

This edition first published in 2015 by Bellwether Media, Inc.

No part of this publication may be reproduced in whole or in part without written permission of the publisher. For information regarding permission, write to Bellwether Media, Inc., Attention: Permissions Department, 5357 Penn Avenue South, Minneapolis, MN 55419.

Library of Congress Cataloging-in-Publication Data

Green, Sara, 1964- author.
  Jeff Bezos / by Sara Green.
      pages cm. – (Pilot. Tech Icons)
  Summary: "Engaging images accompany information about Jeff Bezos. The combination of high-interest subject matter and narrative text is intended for students in grades 3 through 7"– Provided by publisher.
  Audience: Ages 7-12.
  Includes bibliographical references and index.
  ISBN 978-1-60014-989-4 (hardcover : alk. paper)
  1. Bezos, Jeffrey–Juvenile literature. 2. Amazon.com (Firm)–Juvenile literature. 3. Internet bookstores–United States– History–Juvenile literature. 4. Electronic commerce–United States–Biography–Juvenile literature. 5. Businessmen–United States–Biography–Juvenile literature. I. Title.
  Z473.B47G74 2014
  381.4500092–dc23
                           2014005985

Printed in the United States of America, North Mankato, MN.

TABLE OF CONTENTS

12:56 PM

amazon.com

CHAPTER 1

WHO IS JEFF BEZOS?

Jeff Bezos gave people a new way to shop. He is the founder and **CEO** of Amazon.com, the largest online store in the world. Customers can buy almost anything on this web site. Jeff's brilliant mind and outstanding leadership skills have brought him great success. In March 2014, he was worth $32 billion. This makes him one of the richest people on Earth. However, Jeff is still dedicated to providing the best customer service possible, both today and in the future. He always thinks about his customers' long-term needs and how to meet them.

Jeff was born on January 12, 1964, in Albuquerque, New Mexico. His parents, Jacklyn and Ted Jorgensen, were only teenagers. Their marriage lasted for less than a year. When Jeff was 4 years old, his mother married Mike Bezos. Mike adopted Jeff and gave him his last name. In 1970, Jeff's sister, Christina, was born. His brother, Mark, was born one year later.

ICON BIO

Name: Jeffrey Preston Bezos

Nickname: Jeff

Birthday: January 12, 1964

Hometown: Albuquerque, New Mexico

Marital status: Married to MacKenzie Bezos since 1993

Children: Three boys and one girl

Hobbies/ Interests: Reading, studying space travel, *Star Trek*

A MECHANICAL WIZARD

The Bezos family moved to Houston, Texas, after Jeff's parents got married. Teachers quickly noticed Jeff's extraordinary intelligence. He was in a program for gifted students at River Oaks Elementary School. Jeff especially enjoyed reading, science, and building models. He also liked figuring out how things worked at home. Jeff was often found working on science projects in the garage. He even set up an alarm system on his bedroom door. It kept his younger siblings out of his room.

As a kid, Jeff spent summers at his grandfather's ranch in Cotulla, Texas. He loved helping his grandfather with ranch work. Jeff learned how to ride horses and brand cattle. He also helped his grandfather repair machines, tractors, and windmills.

A HANDY TODDLER

When Jeff was 3 years old, he tried to take his crib apart with a screwdriver. He wanted to turn it into a real bed.

"Work hard,
have fun,
make history."
— Jeff Bezos

A MEMORY FOR PLAYS

Jeff joined a youth football team when he was a kid. Although he was small, he was made captain of the team. He was the only team member who could remember all the plays.

When Jeff was a teenager, the Bezos family moved to Miami, Florida. There, he continued to work on projects and inventions in the family garage. He enjoyed tinkering with electronics and building robots. He even tried to turn a vacuum cleaner into a **hovercraft**! During this time, Jeff began to develop a great interest in computers.

In high school, Jeff's intelligence and hard work earned him many awards. He was named his school's Best Science Student three years in a row. Jeff was also named Best Math Student twice. As a senior, Jeff won a Silver Knight award for his achievements and community service. Popular with his peers, Jeff was both the president and **valedictorian** of his graduating class. In 1982, Jeff graduated from high school. He was already very driven. His graduation speech talked about his wish to build human **colonies** in space.

CHAPTER 3

A GIFTED LEADER

Jeff started his first business the summer after graduation. He and a friend ran a 10-day education camp for kids. They called it the DREAM Institute. The campers read books, learned practical skills, and discussed science. Jeff's experience as a camp leader inspired him to think of his future. He knew it included becoming an **entrepreneur**.

In the fall of 1982, Jeff entered Princeton University in Princeton, New Jersey. There, he studied computer science and **electrical engineering**. He earned high grades and graduated at the top of his class in 1986. After graduation, Jeff was ready to make his mark on the world. He moved to New York City. There, he became a manager at a new **telecommunications** firm called FITEL. By 1988, he needed a change. Jeff found a management job at a company called Bankers Trust. His technical skills and hard work impressed his bosses. Soon, Jeff was promoted to vice president.

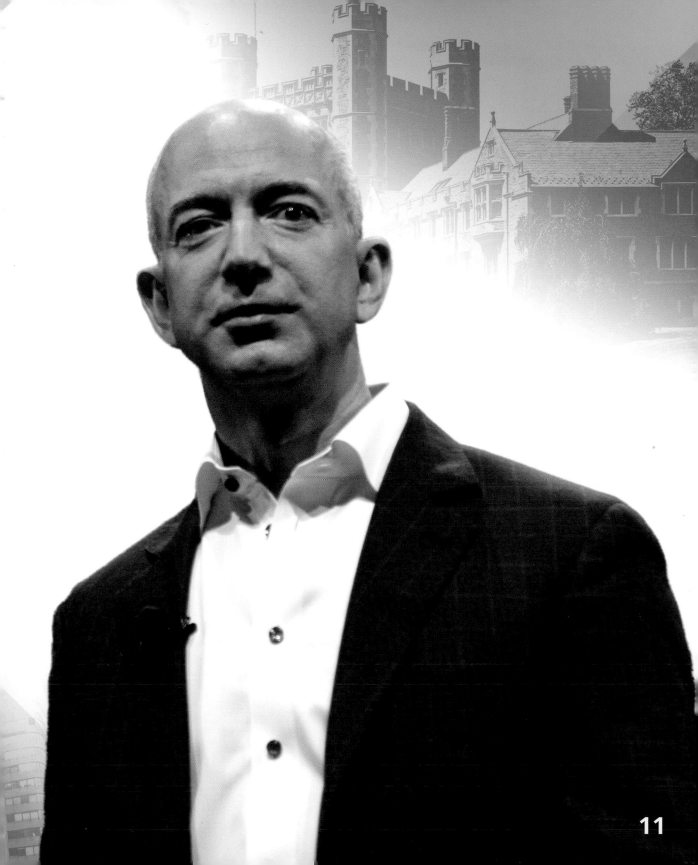

"I knew that if I failed I wouldn't regret that, but I knew the one thing I might regret is not trying."

— Jeff Bezos

ple *want* to read

Jeff had a good job at Bankers Trust, but he was restless. It was time for another change. In 1990, he started a job at an **investment firm** called D.E. Shaw. There, he became the firm's youngest senior vice president. He used his computer skills to help the company **invest** money and trade **stocks**.

During this time, Jeff discovered that people's use of the Internet was growing quickly. He realized it could offer a new way for people to shop. Jeff decided to quit his job to start an online store. After researching many products, he decided to sell books. They had high demand and were cheap to sell. Books were also easy to ship without damage. Jeff set out to create "Earth's Biggest Bookstore." His parents believed in his vision. They gave Jeff $300,000 to start his online bookstore.

I DO!

Jeff met his wife, MacKenzie Tuttle, at D.E. Shaw. She was a research associate in his office. They fell in love and got married in 1993.

13

CHAPTER 4

ONLINE SUCCESS

In 1994, Jeff and his wife, MacKenzie, moved to Seattle, Washington, to develop the online bookstore. Seattle was home to other technology firms. Jeff knew he could find employees with excellent computer skills. Plus, the city was close to a large book **distributor**. At first, Jeff and a few employees worked from his garage. They spent more than a year creating and testing **software**. Finally, in 1995, the web site was ready. Jeff opened his bookstore on July 16. He called it Amazon.com after the river in South America.

At first, many people doubted that Jeff would succeed. They did not think an online bookstore would make money. However, it was very popular from the start. Within 30 days, people from across the world bought books from Amazon. After only two months, Amazon was making $20,000 a week in sales. Within two years, the business outgrew the small garage. It moved to a huge building with two warehouses.

Amazon.com was a success, but Jeff had bigger goals. He was determined to have an online store where people could buy almost everything. In 1998, Jeff began to sell videos, clothes, electronics, and more on Amazon. Customers liked the convenience of shopping online. Jeff's vision was becoming a reality.

Jeff **innovates** to keep his company successful. He continues to add to Amazon's products. In 2007, Amazon began to sell the Kindle, a handheld electronic book reader. Users loved being able to buy, download, and read books on an electronic reader. The original Kindles sold out quickly. Today, the newest version of the Kindle is still as popular as ever.

DRAWING THE LINE
Amazon.com will not sell certain items. These include pets, guns, real estate, and second-hand clothes.

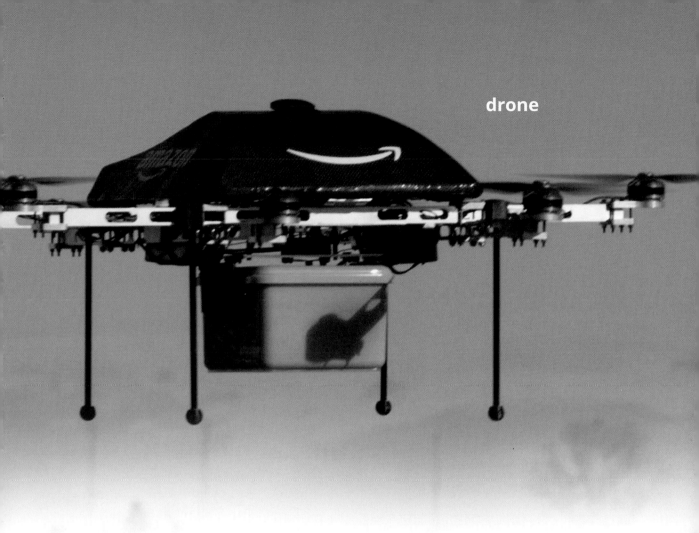

drone

Currently, Jeff is working on a new project called Amazon Prime Air. This service uses **drones** to deliver products to customers in less than 30 minutes. Prime Air is still in the testing stage. However, customers may soon look to the sky to watch their purchases arrive.

CHAPTER 5

FOLLOWING HIS DREAMS

Jeff achieved great success and wealth with Amazon.com. This has allowed him to pursue his longtime dream of space travel. In 2000, he started a company in West Texas called Blue Origin. Its purpose is to build rocket ships at an affordable price. They will carry passengers into space to explore and do research. Passengers will have the adventure of a lifetime! Jeff is also building a 10,000-year clock inside a mountain near Blue Origin. The clock is a symbol for Jeff's long-term thinking. Once completed, it will chime once a year for 10,000 years.

THE FINAL FRONTIER

When he was a child, Jeff dreamed of becoming an astronaut. One of his favorite television shows was *Star Trek*.

In 2013, Jeff purchased *The Washington Post* for $250 million. People read print newspapers less than ever, and this newspaper has been struggling to succeed. With his love for the written word, Jeff is just the person to help a respected newspaper find new life.

RESUME

Education

1982-1986: Princeton University, B.S. in Computer Science and Electrical Engineering (Princeton, New Jersey)

1979-1982: Miami Palmetto High School (Miami, Florida)

Work Experience

2000-present: Founder and owner of Blue Origin

1996-present: CEO of Amazon.com

1994-1996: Developer of Amazon.com

1990-1994: Software developer at D.E. Shaw & Co.; promoted to senior vice president in 1992

1988-1990: Software developer at Bankers Trust; promoted to vice president in 1990

1986-1988: Manager at FITEL

Community Service/Philanthropy

2011: Donated $15 million to the Princeton Neuroscience Institute to study the brain

2011: Donated $10 million to create the Center for Innovation at The Museum of History & Industry in Seattle

2007: Paid $3.98 million for the book *The Tales of Beedle the Bard* by J.K. Rowling to benefit a children's charity

LIFE TIMELINE

January 12, 1964:
Born Jeffrey Preston Jorgensen in Albuquerque, New Mexico

Spring 1982:
Graduates at the top of his class from Miami Palmetto Senior High School in Miami, Florida

1988:
Begins job at Bankers Trust Company

1968:
Adopted by Mike Bezos and name changes to Jeffrey Bezos

Spring 1986:
Graduates from Princeton University with Bachelor of Science degrees in Electrical Engineering and Computer Science; begins job at FITEL

1993:
Marries MacKenzie Tuttle

December 2008:
Named *Publishers Weekly* Person of the Year

amazon

July 1995:
Amazon.com opens for business

December 1999:
Named *Time* magazine's Person of the Year

1994:
Moves to Washington State to develop an online bookstore

August 2013:
Buys *The Washington Post* newspaper

November 2007:
Amazon introduces the Kindle, the first electronic reading device

1990:
Begins job at D.E. Shaw and Co.

April 2014:
Makes *Time* magazine's list of "100 Most Influential People"

May 1997:
Amazon goes public and is worth $438 million

GLOSSARY

CEO—Chief Executive Officer; the CEO is the highest-ranking person in a company.

colonies—distant areas under control by a country where people from that country settle

distributor—a company that supplies stores or businesses with goods

drones—aircraft that fly without pilots

electrical engineering—the study of the design, construction, and uses of technology

entrepreneur—a person who starts a business

hovercraft—a vehicle that moves on a cushion of air

innovates—introduces new ideas about how things can be done

invest—to put money into businesses or ideas

investment firm—a company that puts money into stocks and businesses to make a profit

software—the programs and operating information used by a computer

stocks—shares of ownership in a company

telecommunications—the science of electronic communication across a distance

valedictorian—the top student in a graduating class

TO LEARN MORE

AT THE LIBRARY

Byers, Ann. *Jeff Bezos: The Founder of Amazon.com*. New York, N.Y.: Rosen Pub. Group, 2007.

Landau, Jennifer. *Jeff Bezos and Amazon*. New York, N.Y.: Rosen Pub., 2013.

Robinson, Tom. *Jeff Bezos: Amazon.com Architect*. Edina, Minn.: ABDO Publishing Company, 2010.

ON THE WEB

Learning more about Jeff Bezos is as easy as 1, 2, 3.

1. Go to www.factsurfer.com.

2. Enter "Jeff Bezos" into the search box.

3. Click the "Surf" button and you will see a list of related web sites.

With factsurfer.com, finding more information is just a click away.

INDEX